for Lent 2023

W9-BNK-657

SACRED SPACE

from the website www.sacredspace.ie

Prayer from the Irish Jesuits

LOYOLA PRESS.
A JESUIT MINISTRY

Chicago

LOYOLA PRESS.
A JESUIT MINISTRY

www.loyolapress.com

This edition of *Sacred Space for Lent* is published by arrangement with Messenger Publications, 37 Lower Leeson Street, Dublin D02 W938, Ireland.

Loyola Press in Chicago thanks the Irish Jesuits and Messenger Press for preparing this book for publication.

Cover art credit: beastfromeast/Digital Vision/Getty Images

ISBN-13: 978-0-8294-5535-9

Printed in the United States of America.
22 23 24 25 26 Versa 10 9 8 7 6 5 4 3 2 1

Contents

Sacred Space Prayer

Bless all who worship you, almighty God,
from the rising of the sun to its setting:
from your goodness enrich us,
by your love inspire us,
by your Spirit guide us,
by your power protect us,
in your mercy receive us,
now and always.

How to Use This Booklet

During each week of Lent, begin by reading the section entitled 'Something to think and pray about each day this week'. Then proceed through 'The Presence of God', 'Freedom' and 'Consciousness' steps to prepare yourself to hear the word of God in your heart. In the next step, 'The Word', turn to the Scripture reading for each day of the week. Inspiration points are provided in case you need them. Then return to the 'Conversation' and 'Conclusion' steps. Use this process every day of Lent.

22–25 February 2023

Something to think and pray about each day this week:

The Christian centre is the person of Christ. Our work for Jesus and our love for people, no matter what our calling in life, flow from this. Mother Teresa was once asked why she did what she did, and she simply said 'for Jesus'. This centre always holds, it cannot be unhinged. It is a deeply personal relationship: we are led by Jesus 'one by one', known by name, not as one of a group. We follow him as one we know, not a stranger.

We study his life and times, getting to know the places and events of his life; we become familiar with the gospels and get to know him in the heart. Prayer is the way of keeping our centre of conviction and motivation strong. Freedom grows and we begin to find him everywhere.

Different types of people and spirituality stress different aspects of Jesus. The Eastern approach to Jesus is very much the 'way'; while the African is the 'life'. The European stress is the 'truth'. In Europe we need to rediscover also the joy and vibrancy of the African and Latin American expressions of faith, and also the presence of God in all life's moods and journeys of the Indian and Eastern traditions.

We can get so caught up in small or even big truths and doctrines that we miss other centres of faith. All faith needs the balanced approach to Jesus – way, truth and life.

Donal Neary SJ,
Gospel Reflections for Sundays of Year A

The Presence of God

I pause for a moment
and reflect on God's life-giving presence
in every part of my body,
in everything around me,
in the whole of my life.

Freedom

Many countries are at this moment suffering the agonies of war. I bow my head in thanksgiving for my freedom. I pray for all prisoners and captives.

Consciousness

Knowing that God loves me unconditionally, I look honestly over the past day, its events, and my feelings. Do I have something to be grateful for? Then I give thanks. Is there something I am sorry for? Then I ask forgiveness.

The Word

Now I turn to the Scripture set out for me this day. I read slowly over the words and see if any sentence or sentiment appeals to me.

(Please turn to the Scripture on the following pages. Inspiration points are there, should you need them. When you are ready, return here to continue.)

Conversation

I know with certainty that there were times when you carried me, Lord. There were times when it was through your strength that I got through the dark times in my life.

Conclusion

Glory be to the Father, and to the Son, and to the Holy Spirit,
As it was in the beginning, is now and ever shall be,
World without end. Amen.

Wednesday 22 February
Ash Wednesday

Matthew 6:1–6, 16–18

Jesus said to them, 'Beware of practising your piety before others in order to be seen by them; for then you have no reward from your Father in heaven.

'So whenever you give alms, do not sound a trumpet before you, as the hypocrites do in the synagogues and in the streets, so that they may be praised by others. Truly I tell you, they have received their reward. But when you give alms, do not let your left hand know what your right hand is doing, so that your alms may be done in secret; and your Father who sees in secret will reward you.

'And whenever you pray, do not be like the hypocrites; for they love to stand and pray in the synagogues and at the street corners, so that they may be seen by others. Truly I tell you, they have received their reward. But whenever you pray, go into your room and shut the door and pray to your Father who is in secret; and your Father who sees in secret will reward you.

'And whenever you fast, do not look dismal, like the hypocrites, for they disfigure their faces so as to show others that they are fasting. Truly I tell you, they have received their reward. But when you fast, put oil on your head and wash your face, so that your fasting may be seen not by others but by your Father who is in secret; and your Father who sees in secret will reward you.'

- Religion can be used for selfish reasons, like being well thought of. God asks that we focus on his place in our lives through our faith. We need to recall the priority of God in our lives: that we come from him and go to him, and that he is the companion of our lives.

Thursday 23 February
Luke 9:22–25

Jesus said to his disciples, 'The Son of Man must undergo great suffering, and be rejected by the elders, chief priests and scribes, and be killed, and on the third day be raised.'

Then he said to them all, 'If any want to become my followers, let them deny themselves and take up their cross daily and follow me. For those who want to save their life will lose it, and those who lose their life for my sake will save it. What does it profit them if they gain the whole world, but lose or forfeit themselves?'

- We know from the Gospels that the disciples of Jesus would have been tempted – influenced by the expectation of their fellow Jews – by the prospect of their Master inaugurating a new political and national power. In another Gospel, Peter is roundly denounced by Jesus for attempting to draw him aside from the wholly unexpected path of suffering announced here (making reference to condemned persons often being forced to carry their own cross). We tend in our own minds to catalogue today's passage simply as a prophecy of suffering.

Friday 24 February
Matthew 9:14–15

Then the disciples of John came to him, saying, 'Why do we and the Pharisees fast often, but your disciples do not fast?' And Jesus said to them, 'The wedding-guests cannot mourn as long as the bridegroom is with them, can they? The days will come when the bridegroom is taken away from them, and then they will fast.'

- Jesus is often presented in the gospel as giving his life over to his Father. His convictions and preaching would lead to his death. His future resurrection was in the power of his Father. Much of what we want to hold on to in life can be swiftly taken away – our good health, our security of wealth, even our good name. What we share in love and in God cannot be taken away. Ask in prayer to value love, and to offer your life now and always in love and for love.

Saturday 25 February
Luke 5:27–32

After this he went out and saw a tax-collector named Levi, sitting at the tax booth; and he said to him, 'Follow me.' And he got up, left everything and followed him.

Then Levi gave a great banquet for him in his house; and there was a large crowd of tax-collectors and others sitting at the table with them. The Pharisees and their scribes were complaining to his disciples, saying, 'Why do you eat and drink with tax-collectors and sinners?' Jesus answered, 'Those who are well have no need of a physician, but those who are sick; I have come to call not the righteous but sinners to repentance.'

- Where are the Levis in my world? The drug-pushers, paedophiles, wife-batterers, rapists, those who cheat on tax or social welfare, those who are headlined for hatred in the tabloid press. Lord, these are the sick who need you as physician. Can I help you to reach out to them?

The First Week of Lent
26 February–4 March 2023

Something to think and pray about each day this week:

The days of spring lengthen and Lent echoes nature, inviting us as well to a new springtime of faith. As in farming and gardening, there is work to be done if new growth is to flourish or even to happen at all. We have to look back and see what has done well and what has, in effect, died off. We need to make space by clearing the ground and looking at ourselves honestly. It would be good to identify what will feed and sustain us during this journey from the ashes of Ash Wednesday to the new birth of Easter.

Kieran J. O'Mahony OSA,
Hearers of the Word: Praying and Exploring the Readings for Lent and Holy Week

The Presence of God

I pause for a moment and think of the love and the grace that God showers on me. I am created in the image and likeness of God; I am God's dwelling place.

Freedom

Lord, you granted me the great gift of freedom. In these times, O Lord, grant that I may be free from any form of racism or intolerance. Remind me that we are all equal in your loving eyes.

Consciousness

Knowing that God loves me unconditionally, I can afford to be honest about how I am. How has the day been, and how do I feel now? I share my feelings openly with the Lord.

The Word

I take my time to read the word of God slowly, a few times, allowing myself to dwell on anything that strikes me.

(Please turn to the Scripture on the following pages. Inspiration points are there, should you need them. When you are ready, return here to continue.)

Conversation

Sometimes I wonder what I might say if I were to meet you in person, Lord. I think I might say, 'Thank you' because you are always there for me.

Conclusion
I thank God for these moments we have spent together and for any insights I have been given concerning the text.

Sunday 26 February
First Sunday of Lent
Matthew 4:1–11

Then Jesus was led up by the Spirit into the wilderness to be tempted by the devil. He fasted for forty days and forty nights, and afterwards he was famished. The tempter came and said to him, 'If you are the Son of God, command these stones to become loaves of bread.' But he answered, 'It is written,

> "One does not live by bread alone,
>> but by every word that comes from the
>> mouth of God.""

Then the devil took him to the holy city and placed him on the pinnacle of the temple, saying to him, 'If you are the Son of God, throw yourself down; for it is written,

> "He will command his angels concerning you",
>> and "On their hands they will bear you up,
> so that you will not dash your foot against a
>> stone."'

Jesus said to him, 'Again it is written, "Do not put the Lord your God to the test."'

Again, the devil took him to a very high mountain and showed him all the kingdoms of the world and their splendour; and he said to him, 'All these I will give you, if you will fall down and worship me.' Jesus said to him, 'Away with you, Satan! for it is written,

> "Worship the Lord your God,
>   and serve only him."'

Then the devil left him, and suddenly angels came and waited on him.

- What is the spirit trying to tell me in this story? Am I aware of my own particular 'temptations' that make trouble for me in my life? Do I find wisdom and guidance in Scripture to help me cope with difficulties in my life? Let us consider where Jesus found inspiration and guidance throughout his life.

Monday 27 February
Matthew 25:31–46

Jesus said to them, 'When the Son of Man comes in his glory, and all the angels with him, then he will sit on the throne of his glory. All the nations will be gathered before him, and he will separate people one from another as a shepherd separates the sheep from the goats, and he will put the sheep at his right hand and the goats at the left. Then the king will say to those at his right hand, "Come, you that are blessed by my Father, inherit the kingdom prepared for you from the foundation of the world; for I was hungry and you gave me food, I was thirsty and you gave me something to drink, I was a stranger and you welcomed me, I was naked and you gave me clothing, I was sick and you took care of me, I was in prison and you visited me." Then the righteous will answer him, "Lord, when was it that we saw you hungry and gave you food, or thirsty and gave you something to drink? And when was it that we saw you a stranger and welcomed you, or naked and gave you clothing? And when was it that we saw you sick or in prison and visited you?" And the king will answer them, "Truly I tell you, just as you did it to one of the least of these who are members of my family, you did it to me." Then he will say to those at his left hand, "You that are accursed, depart from me into the eternal fire prepared for the devil and his angels; for I was hungry and you gave me no food, I was thirsty and you gave me nothing to drink, I was a stranger and you did not welcome me, naked and you did not give me clothing, sick and in prison and you did not visit me." Then they also will answer, "Lord, when was it that we saw you hungry or thirsty or a stranger or naked or sick or in prison, and did not take care of you?" Then he will answer them, "Truly I tell you, just as you did not do it to one of the least of these, you did not do it to me." And these will go away into eternal punishment, but the righteous into eternal life.'

- The things we are asked to do are so simple: give food and drink to 'Jesus' in those who are hungry and thirsty; to clothe 'Jesus' in those who are naked; to visit 'Jesus' in those who are sick and in jail. Whether we realise it or not, every time we spontaneously take care of a brother or sister in need it is Jesus himself we are serving.

Tuesday 28 February
Matthew 6:7–15

Jesus said to them, 'When you are praying, do not heap up empty phrases as the Gentiles do; for they think that they will be heard because of their many words. Do not be like them, for your Father knows what you need before you ask him.

'Pray then in this way:
Our Father in heaven,
    hallowed be your name.
    Your kingdom come.
    Your will be done,
        on earth as it is in heaven.
    Give us this day our daily bread.
    And forgive us our debts,
        as we also have forgiven our debtors.
    And do not bring us to the time of trial,
        but rescue us from the evil one.

For if you forgive others their trespasses, your heavenly Father will also forgive you; but if you do not forgive others, neither will your Father forgive your trespasses.'

- The Our Father is so familiar it is hard to be really present to the words we say. Maybe try to just focus on one phrase like 'hallowed be your name'. What is this phrase saying to me right now?

- How might 'hallowing his name' look in my life today? Which phrases in the Our Father give me the greatest comfort and the greatest challenge?

Wednesday 1 March
Luke 11:29–32

When the crowds were increasing, he began to say, 'This generation is an evil generation; it asks for a sign, but no sign will be given to it except the sign of Jonah. For just as Jonah became a sign to the people of Nineveh, so the Son of Man will be to this generation. The queen of the South will rise at the judgement with the people of this generation and condemn them, because she came from the ends of the earth to listen to the wisdom of Solomon, and see, something greater than Solomon is here! The people of Nineveh will rise up at the judgement with this generation and condemn it, because they repented at the proclamation of Jonah, and see, something greater than Jonah is here!'

- Where do I see 'signs' of God's activity in my life? Maybe in nature; family; friends; random acts of kindness; poverty; the homeless?

- 'Something greater than Solomon is here'. Do I catch glimpses of this reality? Help me to have eyes to see and a heart open enough to allow me to become aware of your presence and action in my life.

Thursday 2 March
Matthew 7:7–11

Jesus said, 'Ask, and it will be given to you; search, and you will find; knock, and the door will be opened for you. For everyone who asks receives, and everyone who searches finds, and for everyone who knocks, the door will be opened. Is there anyone among you who, if your child asks for bread, will give a stone? Or if the child asks for a fish, will give a snake? If you then, who are evil, know how to give good gifts to your children, how much more will your Father in heaven give good things to those who ask him!'

- Prayer is never wasted. Good things come in prayer, but perhaps not what someone asks for. Prayer opens the heart for good things from God. Be grateful at the end of prayer for time spent with the God of all goodness. Prayer time is always productive time in making us people of more love.

Friday 3 March
Matthew 5:20–26

Jesus said to the crowds, 'For I tell you, unless your righteousness exceeds that of the scribes and Pharisees, you will never enter the kingdom of heaven.

'You have heard that it was said to those of ancient times, "You shall not murder"; and "whoever murders shall be liable to judgement." But I say to you that if you are angry with a brother or sister, you will be liable to judgement; and if you insult a brother or sister, you will be liable to the council; and if you say, "You fool", you will be liable to the hell of fire. So when you are offering your gift at the altar, if you remember that your brother or sister has something against you, leave your gift there before the altar and go; first be reconciled to your brother or sister, and then come and offer your gift. Come to terms quickly with your accuser while you are on the way to court with him, or your accuser may hand you over to the judge, and the judge to the guard, and you will be thrown into prison. Truly I tell you, you will never get out until you have paid the last penny.'

- Any illusion that Christianity is an 'easy' religion is dispelled here. Can I put any of these teachings of Jesus into action in my own life?

- Do I ever call myself a fool!? Let me not be too hard on myself today. I will ask Jesus to give me the grace to accept myself as I am.

Saturday 4 March
Matthew 5:43–48

Jesus taught them, saying, 'You have heard that it was said, "You shall love your neighbour and hate your enemy." But I say to you, Love your enemies and pray for those who persecute you, so that you may be children of your Father in heaven; for he makes his sun rise on the evil and on the good, and sends rain on the righteous and on the unrighteous. For if you love those who love you, what reward do you have? Do not even the tax-collectors do the same? And if you greet only your brothers and sisters, what more are you doing than others? Do not even the Gentiles do the same? Be perfect, therefore, as your heavenly Father is perfect.'

- As I sit with these lines what is my gut reaction? Is this a 'hard saying' for me? Can I even believe that it is possible for me? Is it good for me? I talk to Jesus about what is going on in my heart now.

- He, Jesus, loved till the end. I am called to be like him. Have I ever experienced the effect of actually praying for whoever has hurt me, to wish them well, wish them peace and healing?

The Second Week of Lent
5–11 March 2023

Something to think and pray about each day this week:

Jesus says to his disciples: 'It is easier for a camel to pass through the eye of a needle than for someone rich to enter the kingdom of God' (Mark 10:25). With this Jesus puts his finger on a central aspect of Christian life: our willingness to become empty or to become poor before God. The disciples are shocked because they sense how difficult it is to be really empty and poor. This is the passage that, time and again, leads to misunderstandings: should we all be poor, not own anything, be ascetic? Does Jesus begrudge us everything? It is he who has promised us a life in fullness. The word 'emptiness' is not easily understood because it can be interpreted in so many different ways. For one thing it sounds negative. Yet it is exactly our willingness to become empty that is essential for our spiritual life. This is why it plays an integral role in contemplative retreats.

Joachim Hartmann and
Annette Clara Unkelhäußer,
Joy in God: Rekindling an Inner Fire

The Presence of God

Dear Jesus, today I call on you, but not to ask for anything. I'd like only to dwell in your presence. May my heart respond to your love.

Freedom

God my creator, you gave me life and the gift of freedom. Through your love I exist in this world. May I never take the gift of life for granted. May I always respect others' right to life.

Consciousness

I ask how I am today. Am I particularly tired, stressed or anxious? If any of these characteristics apply, can I try to let go of the concerns that disturb me?

The Word

The word of God comes down to us through the Scriptures. May the Holy Spirit enlighten my mind and my heart to respond to the gospel teachings.
(Please turn to the Scripture on the following pages. Inspiration points are there, should you need them. When you are ready, return here to continue.)

Conversation

I begin to talk with Jesus about the Scripture I have just read. What part of it strikes a chord in me? Perhaps the words of a friend – or some story I have heard recently – will rise to the surface in my consciousness. If so, does the story throw light on what the Scripture passage may be saying to me?

Conclusion

Glory be to the Father, and to the Son, and to the Holy Spirit,
As it was in the beginning, is now and ever shall be,
World without end. Amen.

Sunday 5 March
Second Sunday of Lent
Matthew 17:1–9

Six days later, Jesus took with him Peter and James and his brother John and led them up a high mountain, by themselves. And he was transfigured before them, and his face shone like the sun, and his clothes became dazzling white. Suddenly there appeared to them Moses and Elijah, talking with him. Then Peter said to Jesus, 'Lord, it is good for us to be here; if you wish, I will make three dwellings here, one for you, one for Moses, and one for Elijah.' While he was still speaking, suddenly a bright cloud overshadowed them, and from the cloud a voice said, 'This is my Son, the Beloved; with him I am well pleased; listen to him!' When the disciples heard this, they fell to the ground and were overcome by fear. But Jesus came and touched them, saying, 'Get up and do not be afraid.' And when they looked up, they saw no one except Jesus himself alone.

As they were coming down the mountain, Jesus ordered them, 'Tell no one about the vision until after the Son of Man has been raised from the dead.'

- The disciples see Jesus revealed in all his divine glory. It is a special moment for them, as Peter confirms – 'it is good for us to be here'.

- Go with the disciples and our Lord, paying close attention to what they say and do. What would they have said to one another after the incident? Imagine one of them in later life giving an account and explanation of the incident.

Monday 6 March
Luke 6:36–38

Jesus said to his disciples, 'Be merciful, just as your Father is merciful.

'Do not judge, and you will not be judged; do not condemn, and you will not be condemned. Forgive, and you will be forgiven; give, and it will be given to you. A good measure, pressed down, shaken together, running over, will be put into your lap; for the measure you give will be the measure you get back.'

- Jesus invites us to be as God is – nothing less! He does not intend to overwhelm us or cause us to feel frustrated by such an enormous invitation, but wants us to wonder at the immensity of God's capacity to love. In our humanity, we are not infinite, but we are called to great love and hope. The invitation reaches to us as we are in our lives, calling us into the life of God.

- Judgement, condemnation and lack of forgiveness inhibit good and bind up the spirit. Lord help me to be generous, not by forcing anything from my-self, but by sharing fully what you give to me.

Tuesday 7 March
Matthew 23:1–12

Then Jesus said to the crowds and to his disciples, 'The scribes and the Pharisees sit on Moses' seat; therefore, do whatever they teach you and follow it; but do not do as they do, for they do not practise what they teach. They tie up heavy burdens, hard to bear, and lay them on the shoulders of others; but they themselves are unwilling to lift a finger to move them. They do all their deeds to be seen by others; for they make their phylacteries broad and their fringes long. They love to have the place of honour at ban-quets and the best seats in the synagogues, and to be greeted with respect in the market-places, and to have people call them rabbi. But you are not to be called rabbi, for you have one teacher, and you are all stu-dents. And call no one your father on earth, for you have one Father – the one in heaven. Nor are you to be called instructors, for you have one instructor, the Messiah. The greatest among you will be your ser-vant. All who exalt themselves will be humbled, and all who humble themselves will be exalted.'

- Christianity should not be a wearying load to carry. Jesus, who said, 'My yoke is easy and my burden is light', was conscious of people's limitations. When I am tempted to pass judgement on another person's perceived failures, do I exercise the same compassion that Jesus did?

Wednesday 8 March
Matthew 20:17–28

While Jesus was going up to Jerusalem, he took the twelve disciples aside by themselves, and said to them on the way, 'See, we are going up to Jerusalem, and the Son of Man will be handed over to the chief priests and scribes, and they will condemn him to death; then they will hand him over to the Gentiles to be mocked and flogged and crucified; and on the third day he will be raised.'

Then the mother of the sons of Zebedee came to him with her sons, and kneeling before him, she asked a favour of him. And he said to her, 'What do you want?' She said to him, 'Declare that these two sons of mine will sit, one at your right hand and one at your left, in your kingdom.' But Jesus answered, 'You do not know what you are asking. Are you able to drink the cup that I am about to drink?' They said to him, 'We are able.' He said to them, 'You will indeed drink my cup, but to sit at my right hand and at my left, this is not mine to grant, but it is for those for whom it has been prepared by my Father.'

When the ten heard it, they were angry with the two brothers. But Jesus called them to him and said, 'You know that the rulers of the Gentiles lord it over them, and their great ones are tyrants over them. It will not be so among you; but whoever wishes to be great among you must be your servant, and whoever wishes to be first among you must be your slave; just as the Son of Man came not to be served but to serve, and to give his life a ransom for many.'

- To love is to serve. To love is to be called to go beyond myself and my needs for others. Jesus came among us to teach us how to live a fully human life.

- Have you ever experienced that 'going beyond' yourself for others? Talk to Jesus about this experience.

Thursday 9 March
Luke 16:19–31

Then Jesus said to his disciples, 'There was a rich man who was dressed in purple and fine linen and who feasted sumptuously every day. And at his gate lay a poor man named Lazarus, covered with sores, who longed to satisfy his hunger with what fell from the rich man's table; even the dogs would come and lick his sores. The poor man died and was carried away by the angels to be with Abraham. The rich man also died and was buried. In Hades, where he was being tormented, he looked up and saw Abraham far away with Lazarus by his side. He called out, "Father Abraham, have mercy on me, and send Lazarus to dip the tip of his finger in water and cool my tongue; for I am in agony in these flames." But Abraham said, "Child, remember that during your lifetime you received your good things, and Lazarus in like manner evil things; but now he is comforted here, and you are in agony. Besides all this, between you and us a great chasm has been fixed, so that those who might want to pass from here to you cannot do so, and no one can cross from there to us." He said, "Then, father, I beg you to send him to my father's house – for I have five brothers – that he may warn them, so that they will not also come into this place of torment." Abraham replied, "They have Moses and the prophets; they should listen to them." He said, "No, father Abraham; but if someone goes to them from the dead, they will repent." He said to him, "If they do not listen to Moses and the prophets, neither will they be convinced even if someone rises from the dead.'"

- This story reminds us of the huge inequality of people in Jesus' time and still today. The parable invites us to see ourselves as richer in the goods of the world than many millions. Even by having access to this text, you count among the privileged world. Praying on this story will simply challenge us into care for the needy, and, in whatever way we can, to improve the lives of very poor people.

Friday 10 March
Matthew 21:33–43, 45–46

Jesus said to them, 'Listen to another parable. There was a landowner who planted a vineyard, put a fence around it, dug a wine press in it, and built a watch-tower. Then he leased it to tenants and went to another country. When the harvest time had come, he sent his slaves to the tenants to collect his produce. But the tenants seized his slaves and beat one, killed another, and stoned another. Again he sent other slaves, more than the first; and they treated them in the same way. Finally he sent his son to them, saying, "They will respect my son." But when the tenants saw the son, they said to themselves, "This is the heir; come, let us kill him and get his inheritance." So they seized him, threw him out of the vineyard, and killed him. Now when the owner of the vineyard comes, what will he do to those tenants?' They said to him, 'He will put those wretches to a miserable death, and lease the vineyard to other tenants who will give him the produce at the harvest time.'

Jesus said to them, 'Have you never read in the scriptures:

"The stone that the builders rejected
   has become the cornerstone;
this was the Lord's doing,
   and it is amazing in our eyes"?

Therefore I tell you, the kingdom of God will be taken away from you and given to a people that produces the fruits of the kingdom.'

When the chief priests and the Pharisees heard his parables, they realised that he was speaking about them. They wanted to arrest him, but they feared the crowds, because they regarded him as a prophet.

• Jesus – the Son – comes to us so that we might receive our inheritance; we do not need to take anything by force, but can trust in Jesus' promise, message and presence.

Saturday 11 March
Luke 15:1–3, 11–32

Now all the tax-collectors and sinners were coming near to listen to him. And the Pharisees and the scribes were grumbling and saying, 'This fellow welcomes sinners and eats with them.'

So he told them this parable: 'There was a man who had two sons. The younger of them said to his father, "Father, give me the share of the property that will belong to me." So he divided his property between them. A few days later the younger son gathered all he had and travelled to a distant country, and there he squandered his property in dissolute living. When he had spent everything, a severe famine took place throughout that country, and he began to be in need. So he went and hired himself out to one of the citizens of that country, who sent him to his fields to feed the pigs. He would gladly have filled himself with the pods that the pigs were eating; and no one gave him anything. But when he came to himself he said, "How many of my father's hired hands have bread enough and to spare, but here I am dying of hunger! I will get up and go to my father, and I will say to him, 'Father, I have sinned against heaven and before you; I am no longer worthy to be called your son; treat me like one of your hired hands.'" So he set off and went to his father. But while he was still far off, his father saw him and was filled with compassion; he ran and put his arms around him and kissed him. Then the son said to him, "Father, I have sinned against heaven and before you; I am no longer worthy to be called your son." But the father said to his slaves, "Quickly, bring out a robe – the best one – and put it on him; put a ring on his finger and sandals on his feet. And get the fatted calf and kill it, and let us eat and celebrate; for this son of mine was dead and is alive again; he was lost and is found!" And they began to celebrate.

'Now his elder son was in the field; and when he came and approached the house, he heard music and dancing. He called one of the slaves and asked what was going on. He replied, "Your brother has come, and your father has killed the fatted calf, because he has got him back safe and sound." Then he became angry and refused to go in. His father came out and began to plead with him. But he answered his father, "Listen! For all these years I have been working like a slave for you, and I have never disobeyed your command; yet you have never given me even a young goat so that I might celebrate with my friends. But when this son of yours came back, who has devoured your property with prostitutes, you killed the fatted calf for him!" Then the father said to him, "Son, you are always with me, and all that is mine is yours. But we had to celebrate and rejoice, because this brother of yours was dead and has come to life; he was lost and has been found."'

- This classic parable has a universal appeal. The figures of the father and his two sons are portrayed vividly and memorably. The description of the relationships between them is psychologically acute. The central character is the father; it is he who is 'prodigal', not his younger son. The prodigality of the father's love is boundless and unconditional.

The Third Week of Lent
12–18 March 2023

Something to think and pray about each day this week:

We live in a very noisy, busy world, a culture marked by constant distraction. Even at the ordinary level of relationship, attending to the other – really hearing him or her – is a challenge. It happens when we choose to make space, to shut out the other noises and graciously attend to each other. Something similar may be said of the life of the spirit. Listening to the Son happens when we choose it and, by means of practical choices, create spaces in our lives for such encounters.

Kieran J. O'Mahony OSA,
*Hearers of the Word: Praying and Exploring the
Readings for Lent and Holy Week*

The Presence of God

God is with me, but even more astounding, God is within me.

Let me dwell for a moment on God's life-giving presence

in my body, in my mind, in my heart,

as I sit here, right now.

Freedom

Lord, may I never take the gift of freedom for granted. You gave me the great blessing of freedom of spirit. Fill my spirit with your peace and joy.

Consciousness

I remind myself that I am in the presence of God, who is my strength in times of weakness and my comforter in times of sorrow.

The Word

I take my time to read the word of God slowly, a few times, allowing myself to dwell on anything that strikes me.

(Please turn to the Scripture on the following pages. Inspiration points are there, should you need them. When you are ready, return here to continue.)

Conversation

Jesus, you always welcomed little children when you walked on this earth. Teach me to have a childlike trust in you. Teach me to live in the knowledge that you will never abandon me.

Conclusion

Glory be to the Father, and to the Son, and to the Holy Spirit,

As it was in the beginning, is now and ever shall be, World without end. Amen.

Sunday 12 March
Third Sunday of Lent
John 4:5–42

So he came to a Samaritan city called Sychar, near the plot of ground that Jacob had given to his son Joseph. Jacob's well was there, and Jesus, tired out by his journey, was sitting by the well. It was about noon.

A Samaritan woman came to draw water, and Jesus said to her, 'Give me a drink'. (His disciples had gone to the city to buy food.) The Samaritan woman said to him, 'How is it that you, a Jew, ask a drink of me, a woman of Samaria?' (Jews do not share things in common with Samaritans.) Jesus answered her, 'If you knew the gift of God, and who it is that is saying to you, "Give me a drink", you would have asked him, and he would have given you living water.' The woman said to him, 'Sir, you have no bucket, and the well is deep. Where do you get that living water? Are you greater than our ancestor Jacob, who gave us the well, and with his sons and his flocks drank from it?' Jesus said to her, 'Everyone who drinks of this water will be thirsty again, but those who drink of the water that I will give them will never be thirsty. The water that I will give will become in them a spring of water gushing up to eternal life.' The woman said to him, 'Sir, give me this water, so that I may never be thirsty or have to keep coming here to draw water.'

Jesus said to her, 'Go, call your husband, and come back.' The woman answered him, 'I have no husband.' Jesus said to her, 'You are right in saying, "I have no husband"; for you have had five husbands, and the one you have now is not your husband. What you have said is true!' The woman said to him, 'Sir, I see that you are a prophet. Our ancestors worshipped on this mountain, but you say that the place where people must worship is in Jerusalem.' Jesus said to her, 'Woman, believe me, the hour is coming when you will worship the Father neither on this mountain nor in Jerusalem. You worship what you do not know; we worship what we know, for salvation is from the Jews. But the hour is coming, and is now here, when the true worshippers will worship the Father in spirit and truth, for the Father seeks such as these to worship him. God is spirit, and those who worship him must worship in spirit and truth.' The woman said to him, 'I know that Messiah is coming' (who is called Christ). 'When he comes, he will proclaim all things to us.' Jesus said to her, 'I am he, the one who is speaking to you.'

Just then his disciples came. They were astonished that he was speaking with a woman, but no one said, 'What do you want?' or, 'Why are you speaking with her?' Then the woman left her water-jar and went back to the city. She said to the people, 'Come and see a man who told me everything I have ever done!

He cannot be the Messiah, can he?' They left the city and were on their way to him.

Meanwhile the disciples were urging him, 'Rabbi, eat something.' But he said to them, 'I have food to eat that you do not know about.' So the disciples said to one another, 'Surely no one has brought him something to eat?' Jesus said to them, 'My food is to do the will of him who sent me and to complete his work. Do you not say, "Four months more, then comes the harvest"? But I tell you, look around you, and see how the fields are ripe for harvesting. The reaper is already receiving wages and is gathering fruit for eternal life, so that sower and reaper may rejoice together. For here the saying holds true, "One sows and another reaps." I sent you to reap that for which you did not labour. Others have laboured, and you have entered into their labour.'

Many Samaritans from that city believed in him because of the woman's testimony, 'He told me everything I have ever done.' So when the Samaritans came to him, they asked him to stay with them; and he stayed there for two days. And many more believed because of his word. They said to the woman, 'It is no longer because of what you said that we believe, for we have heard for ourselves, and we know that this is truly the Saviour of the world.'

- Lord, I am going about my business like the Samaritan woman, and am taken aback when you accost me at the well. You interrupt my business, my getting and spending, and the routines of my day. Let me savour this encounter, imagine you probing my desires, showing you know the waywardness of my heart. At the end, like her, I am moved with such joy at meeting you that I cannot keep it to myself.

Monday 13 March
Luke 4:24–30

And he said, 'Truly I tell you, no prophet is accepted in the prophet's home town. But the truth is, there were many widows in Israel in the time of Elijah, when the heaven was shut up for three years and six months, and there was a severe famine over all the land; yet Elijah was sent to none of them except to a widow at Zarephath in Sidon. There were also many lepers in Israel in the time of the prophet Elisha, and none of them was cleansed except Naaman the Syrian.' When they heard this, all in the synagogue were filled with rage. They got up, drove him out of the town, and led him to the brow of the hill on which their town was built, so that they might hurl him off the cliff. But he passed through the midst of them and went on his way.

• This is about the expectation of miracles and cures. The self-important Naaman feels he has been slighted: he meets only a messenger, not the prophet himself; and the cure depends on Naaman washing himself in the river, instead of receiving hands-on treatment by Elisha.

- I am the same, Lord. Even in my neediness my ego pushes through. I want to be not just a victim but a celebrity victim. I want not just a cure, but to be the centre of attention. Help me to centre on you, not on me.

Tuesday 14 March
Matthew 18:21–35

Then Peter came and said to him, 'Lord, if another member of the church sins against me, how often should I forgive? As many as seven times?' Jesus said to him, 'Not seven times, but, I tell you, seventy-seven times.

'For this reason the kingdom of heaven may be compared to a king who wished to settle accounts with his slaves. When he began the reckoning, one who owed him ten thousand talents was brought to him; and, as he could not pay, his lord ordered him to be sold, together with his wife and children and all his possessions, and payment to be made. So the slave fell on his knees before him, saying, "Have patience with me, and I will pay you everything." And out of pity for him, the lord of that slave released him and forgave him the debt. But that same slave, as he went out, came upon one of his fellow-slaves who owed him a hundred denarii; and seizing him by the throat, he said, "Pay what you owe." Then his fellow-slave fell down and pleaded with him, "Have patience with me, and I will pay you." But he refused; then he went and threw him into prison until he should pay the debt. When his fellow-slaves saw what had happened, they were greatly distressed, and they went and reported to their lord all that had taken place. Then his lord summoned him and said to him, "You wicked slave! I forgave you all that debt because you pleaded with me. Should you not have had mercy on your fellow-slave, as I had mercy on you?" And in anger his lord handed him over to be tortured until he should pay his entire debt. So my heavenly Father will also do to every one of you, if you do not forgive your brother or sister from your heart.'

- As Jesus continues to emphasise forgiveness, I humbly bring myself before God who forgives me everything, who loves me beyond any sin. The forgiveness that God gives is often difficult for me to receive. I think of how it is given generously to me so that I may give it freely to others.

- I pray for those who have caused me hurt and, even if I can't wish them well now, I pray that one day I might.

Wednesday 15 March
Matthew 5:17–19

Jesus said to his disciples, 'Do not think that I have come to abolish the law or the prophets; I have come not to abolish but to fulfil. For truly I tell you, until heaven and earth pass away, not one letter, not one stroke of a letter, will pass from the law until all is accomplished. Therefore, whoever breaks one of the least of these commandments, and teaches others to do the same, will be called least in the kingdom of heaven; but whoever does them and teaches them will be called great in the kingdom of heaven.'

• I consider how it is that my way of living has an influence on others. I pray in thanksgiving for those places in my life in which I can imagine that I have a good influence. I ask God's help in the areas in which my example and inspiration might be better.

Thursday 16 March
Luke 11:14–23

Now he was casting out a demon that was mute; when the demon had gone out, the one who had been mute spoke, and the crowds were amazed. But some of them said, 'He casts out demons by Beelzebul, the ruler of the demons.' Others, to test him, kept demanding from him a sign from heaven. But he knew what they were thinking and said to them, 'Every kingdom divided against itself becomes a desert, and house falls on house. If Satan also is divided against himself, how will his kingdom stand? – for you say that I cast out the demons by Beelzebul. Now if I cast out the demons by Beelzebul, by whom do your exorcists cast them out? Therefore they will be your judges. But if it is by the finger of God that I cast out the demons, then the kingdom of God has come to you. When a strong man, fully armed, guards his castle, his property is safe. But when one stronger than he attacks him and overpowers him, he takes away his armour in which he trusted and divides his plunder. Whoever is not with me is against me, and whoever does not gather with me scatters.'

- You know how painful it is if your motives are misunderstood, if a twisted interpretation is put on your good intentions. Such experiences help you identify with Jesus and feel with him. Be there with him; share your experiences with him.

Friday 17 March
St Patrick, Bishop and Patron of Ireland
Mark 12:28–34

One of the scribes came near and heard them disputing with one another, and seeing that he answered them well, he asked him, 'Which commandment is the first of all?' Jesus answered, 'The first is, "Hear,

O Israel: the Lord our God, the Lord is one; you shall love the Lord your God with all your heart, and with all your soul, and with all your mind, and with all your strength." The second is this, "You shall love your neighbour as yourself." There is no other commandment greater than these.' Then the scribe said to him, 'You are right, Teacher; you have truly said that "he is one, and besides him there is no other"; and "to love him with all the heart, and with all the understanding, and with all the strength", and "to love one's neighbour as oneself", – this is much more important than all whole burnt-offerings and sacrifices.' When Jesus saw that he answered wisely, he said to him, 'You are not far from the kingdom of God.' After that no one dared to ask him any question.

• 'Love your neighbour as yourself' – just how do I love myself? I am not just aware of present pleasure or pain. I think ahead, protect my routines and give energy to ensuring my comfort. Lord, if you are asking me to do all that for my neighbour, I will need to try much harder than I am doing.

Saturday 18 March
Luke 18:9–14

He also told this parable to some who trusted in themselves that they were righteous and regarded others with contempt: 'Two men went up to the temple to pray, one a Pharisee and the other a tax-collector. The Pharisee, standing by himself, was praying thus, "God, I thank you that I am not like other people: thieves, rogues, adulterers, or even like this tax-collector. I fast twice a week; I give a tenth of all my income." But the tax-collector, standing far off, would not even look up to heaven, but was beating his breast and saying, "God, be merciful to me, a sinner!" I tell you, this man went down to his home justified rather than the other; for all who exalt themselves will be humbled, but all who humble themselves will be exalted.'

- Am I shocked and scandalised by this parable, or do I discover a Pharisee and a publican in my heart too? Sometimes I cannot avoid feeling morally superior and holier than others, or even to a particular person, however much I try not to. I feel I tick all the boxes, unlike others. I humbly ask for light to see and feel the deep roots pride has in my heart, and for the grace of real humility.

The Fourth Week of Lent
19–25 March

Something to think and pray about each day this week:

Some saw a blind man being cured and walked on amazed. Others saw the same cures and found faith. We can see things – everyday things – with different eyes. A sick woman may be seen with the eye of compassion for illness, hope for a cure, profit for a profession. The Christian tries to see the world with the eye of faith.

We learn to see and love with the eye of faith by looking at the look of Jesus towards us. It is often a big jump to believe in what we cannot see. Jesus looks at each of us with faith in our goodness and with love.

Maybe we can walk around in this atmosphere of faith, 'seeing' God in a flower, in a parent holding a child's hand, in a person pushing a wheelchair with courage, and notice that in many ways God is near and the presence of Jesus is at hand.

Donal Neary SJ,
Gospel Reflections for Sundays of Year A

The Presence of God

Dear Lord, as I come to you today, fill my heart, my whole being, with the wonder of your presence. Help me remain receptive to you as I put aside the cares of this world. Fill my mind with your peace.

Freedom

Lord, grant me the grace to be free from the excesses of this life. Let me not get caught up with the desire for wealth. Keep my heart and mind free to love and serve you.

Consciousness

I exist in a web of relationships: links to nature, people, God.

I trace out these links, giving thanks for the life that flows through them.

Some links are twisted or broken; I may feel regret, anger, disappointment.

I pray for the gift of acceptance and forgiveness.

The Word

God speaks to each of us individually. I listen attentively to hear what he is saying to me. Read the text a few times, then listen.

(Please turn to the Scripture on the following pages. Inspiration points are there, should you need them. When you are ready, return here to continue.)

Conversation

Jesus, you speak to me through the words of the Gospels. May I respond to your call today. Teach me to recognise your hand at work in my daily living.

Conclusion

I thank God for these moments we have spent together and for any insights I have been given concerning the text.

Sunday 19 March
Fourth Sunday of Lent

John 9:1–41

As he walked along, he saw a man blind from birth. His disciples asked him, 'Rabbi, who sinned, this man or his parents, that he was born blind?' Jesus answered, 'Neither this man nor his parents sinned; he was born blind so that God's works might be revealed in him. We must work the works of him who sent me while it is day; night is coming when no one can work. As long as I am in the world, I am the light of the world.' When he had said this, he spat on the ground and made mud with the saliva and spread the mud on the man's eyes, saying to him, 'Go, wash in the pool of Siloam' (which means Sent). Then he went and washed and came back able to see. The neighbours and those who had seen him before as a beggar began to ask, 'Is this not the man who used to sit and beg?' Some were saying, 'It is he.' Others were saying, 'No, but it is someone like him.' He kept saying, 'I am the man.' But they kept asking him, 'Then how were your eyes opened?' He answered, 'The man called Jesus made mud, spread it on my eyes, and said to me, "Go to Siloam and wash." Then I went and washed and received my sight.' They said to him, 'Where is he?' He said, 'I do not know.'

They brought to the Pharisees the man who had formerly been blind. Now it was a sabbath day when

Jesus made the mud and opened his eyes. Then the Pharisees also began to ask him how he had received his sight. He said to them, 'He put mud on my eyes. Then I washed, and now I see.' Some of the Pharisees said, 'This man is not from God, for he does not observe the sabbath.' But others said, 'How can a man who is a sinner perform such signs?' And they were divided. So they said again to the blind man, 'What do you say about him? It was your eyes he opened.' He said, 'He is a prophet.'

The Jews did not believe that he had been blind and had received his sight until they called the parents of the man who had received his sight and asked them, 'Is this your son, who you say was born blind? How then does he now see?' His parents answered, 'We know that this is our son, and that he was born blind; but we do not know how it is that now he sees, nor do we know who opened his eyes. Ask him; he is of age. He will speak for himself.' His parents said this because they were afraid of the Jews; for the Jews had already agreed that anyone who confessed Jesus to be the Messiah would be put out of the synagogue. Therefore his parents said, 'He is of age; ask him.'

So for the second time they called the man who had been blind, and they said to him, 'Give glory to God! We know that this man is a sinner.' He answered, 'I do not know whether he is a sinner. One thing I do know, that though I was blind, now I see.' They said to him, 'What did he do to you? How did he open your eyes?' He answered them, 'I have told you already, and you would not listen. Why do you want to hear it again? Do you also want to become his disciples?' Then they reviled him, saying, 'You are his disciple, but we are disciples of Moses. We know that God has spoken to Moses, but as for this man, we do not know where he comes from.' The man answered, 'Here is an astonishing thing! You do not know where he comes from, and yet he opened my eyes. We know that God does not listen to sinners, but he does listen to one who worships him and obeys his will. Never since the world began has it been heard that anyone opened the eyes of a person born blind. If this man were not from God, he could do nothing.' They answered him, 'You were born entirely in sins, and are you trying to teach us?' And they drove him out.

Jesus heard that they had driven him out, and when he found him, he said, 'Do you believe in the Son of Man?' He answered, 'And who is he, sir? Tell me, so that I may believe in him.' Jesus said to him, 'You have seen him, and the one speaking with you is he.' He said, 'Lord, I believe.' And he worshipped him. Jesus said, 'I came into this world for judgement so that those who do not see may see, and those who do see may become blind.' Some of the Pharisees near him heard this and said to him, 'Surely we are not blind, are we?' Jesus said to them, 'If you were blind, you would not have sin. But now that you say, "We see", your sin remains.'

• What did he see? His eyes were opened to the light of faith, that Jesus was the Son of man. Can we pray that our eyes are opened to see the face of God in everyone we meet? And in everyone, friend or foe, for whom we pray?

Monday 20 March
St Joseph, Spouse of the Blessed Virgin Mary
Luke 2:41–51

Now every year his parents went to Jerusalem for the festival of the Passover. And when he was twelve years old, they went up as usual for the festival. When the festival was ended and they started to return, the boy Jesus stayed behind in Jerusalem, but his parents did not know it. Assuming that he was in the group of travellers, they went a day's journey. Then they started to look for him among their relatives and friends. When they did not find him, they returned to Jerusalem to search for him. After three days they found him in the temple, sitting among the teachers, listening to them and asking them questions. And all who heard him were amazed at his understanding and his answers. When his parents saw him they were astonished; and his mother said to him, 'Child, why have you treated us like this? Look, your father and I have been searching for you in great anxiety.' He said to them, 'Why were you searching for me? Did you not know that I must be in my Father's house?' But they did not understand what he said to them. Then he went down with them and came to Nazareth, and was obedient to them. His mother treasured all these things in her heart.

- Most people, in one way or another, leave their family environment. While our family always has a central place in our concerns, we are also called to serve the wider family. All of us, and especially Christians, are called to follow the example of Jesus and align ourselves with the family of the world. We are all brothers and sisters to each other and are called to care for and love each other.

Tuesday 21 March
John 5:1–16

After this there was a festival of the Jews, and Jesus went up to Jerusalem.

Now in Jerusalem by the Sheep Gate there is a pool, called in Hebrew Beth-zatha, which has five porticoes. In these lay many invalids – blind, lame, and paralysed. One man was there who had been ill for thirty-eight years. When Jesus saw him lying there and knew that he had been there a long time, he said to him, 'Do you want to be made well?' The sick man answered him, 'Sir, I have no one to put me into the pool when the water is stirred up; and while I am making my way, someone else steps down ahead of me.' Jesus said to him, 'Stand up, take your mat and walk.' At once the man was made well, and he took up his mat and began to walk.

Now that day was a sabbath. So the Jews said to the man who had been cured, 'It is the sabbath; it is not lawful for you to carry your mat.' But he answered them, 'The man who made me well said to me, "Take up your mat and walk."' They asked him, 'Who is the man who said to you, "Take it up and walk"?' Now the man who had been healed did not know who it was, for Jesus had disappeared in the crowd that was there. Later Jesus found him in the temple and said to him, 'See, you have been made well! Do not sin any more, so that nothing worse happens to you.' The man went away and told the Jews that it was Jesus who had made him well. Therefore the Jews started persecuting Jesus, because he was doing such things on the sabbath.

- Are there sick people in your family, among your friends? Bring them, one by one, before the Lord asking him to do what is best for them. Maybe you are worried about your own health? Tell the Lord of your anxieties and leave them with him. 'Cast all your anxiety on him, because he cares for you' (1 Peter 5:7).

- What might the Lord say in response to your prayer?

Wednesday 22 March

John 5:17–30

But Jesus answered them, 'My Father is still working, and I also am working.' For this reason the Jews were seeking all the more to kill him, because he was not only breaking the sabbath, but was also calling God his own Father, thereby making himself equal to God.

Jesus said to them, 'Very truly, I tell you, the Son can do nothing on his own, but only what he sees the Father doing; for whatever the Father does, the Son does likewise. The Father loves the Son and shows him all that he himself is doing; and he will show him greater works than these, so that you will be astonished. Indeed, just as the Father raises the dead and gives them life, so also the Son gives life to whomsoever he wishes. The Father judges no one but has given all judgement to the Son, so that all may honour the Son just as they honour the Father. Anyone who does not honour the Son does not honour the Father who sent him. Very truly, I tell you, anyone who hears my word and believes him who sent me has eternal life, and does not come under judgement, but has passed from death to life.

'Very truly, I tell you, the hour is coming, and is now here, when the dead will hear the voice of the Son of God, and those who hear will live. For just as the Father has life in himself, so he has granted the Son also to have life in himself; and he has given him authority to execute judgement, because he is the Son of Man. Do not be astonished at this; for the hour is coming when all who are in their graves will hear his voice and will come out – those who have done good, to the resurrection of life, and those who have done evil, to the resurrection of condemnation.

'I can do nothing on my own. As I hear, I judge; and my judgement is just, because I seek to do not my own will but the will of him who sent me.'

- The Creator has handed over all judgement to his Son. This means that the words that Jesus speaks judge us. We need to listen to them, accept them deeply and live by them. They show us up – how good or how insensitive and erring we are.

Thursday 23 March
John 5:31–47

Jesus answered them, 'If I testify about myself, my testimony is not true. There is another who testifies on my behalf, and I know that his testimony to me is true. You sent messengers to John, and he testified to the truth. Not that I accept such human testimony, but I say these things so that you may be saved. He was a burning and shining lamp, and you were willing to rejoice for a while in his light. But I have a testimony greater than John's. The works that the Father has given me to complete, the very works that I am doing, testify on my behalf that the Father has sent me. And the Father who sent me has himself testified on my behalf. You have never heard his voice or seen his form, and you do not have his word abiding in you, because you do not believe him whom he has sent.

'You search the scriptures because you think that in them you have eternal life; and it is they that testify on my behalf. Yet you refuse to come to me to have life. I do not accept glory from human beings. But I know that you do not have the love of God in you. I have come in my Father's name, and you do not accept me; if another comes in his own name, you will accept him. How can you believe when you accept glory from one another and do not seek the glory that comes from the one who alone is God? Do not think that I will accuse you before the Father; your accuser is Moses, on whom you have set your hope. If you believed Moses, you would believe me, for he wrote about me. But if you do not believe what he wrote, how will you believe what I say?'

- Thank the Lord for the encouragement that came from home, school and friends. Seek to forgive those who were a source of discouragement.
- Ask for the grace to keep growing in the freedom to be your own person, to speak your truth and witness to the risen Jesus.

Friday 24 March
John 7:1-2, 10, 25–30

After this Jesus went about in Galilee. He did not wish to go about in Judea because the Jews were looking for an opportunity to kill him. Now the Jewish festival of Booths was near.

But after his brothers had gone to the festival, then he also went, not publicly but as it were in secret.

Now some of the people of Jerusalem were saying, 'Is not this the man whom they are trying to kill? And here he is, speaking openly, but they say nothing to him! Can it be that the authorities really know that this is the Messiah? Yet we know where this man is from; but when the Messiah comes, no one will know where he is from.' Then Jesus cried out as he was teaching in the temple, 'You know me, and you know where I am from. I have not come on my own. But the one who sent me is true, and you do not know him. I know him, because I am from him, and he sent me.'

Then they tried to arrest him, but no one laid hands on him, because his hour had not yet come.

• The one who sent Jesus contains all truth. But Jesus himself is that truth. Those who listened to him did not really know what truth is. To accept Jesus is to have the truth at its deepest level.

Saturday 25 March
The Annunciation of the Lord
Luke 1:26–38

In the sixth month the angel Gabriel was sent by God to a town in Galilee called Nazareth, to a virgin engaged to a man whose name was Joseph, of the house of David. The virgin's name was Mary. And he came to her and said, 'Greetings, favoured one! The Lord is with you.' But she was much perplexed by his words and pondered what sort of greeting this might be. The angel said to her, 'Do not be afraid, Mary, for you have found favour with God. And now, you will conceive in your womb and bear a son, and you will name him Jesus. He will be great, and will be called the Son of the Most High, and the Lord God will give to him the throne of his ancestor David. He will reign over the house of Jacob for ever, and of his kingdom there will be no end.' Mary said to the angel, 'How can this be, since I am a virgin?' The angel said to her, 'The Holy Spirit will come upon you, and the power of the Most High will overshadow you; therefore the child to be born will be holy; he will be called Son of God. And now, your relative Elizabeth in her old age has also conceived a son; and this is the sixth month for her who was said to be barren. For nothing will be impossible with God.' Then Mary said, 'Here am I, the servant of the Lord; let it be with me according to your word.' Then the angel departed from her.

- Lord, when the silence seems heavy and impenetrable, I recall how it can be broken at the most unexpected time and in the most unexpected circumstances. Like Mary, I must be still enough to hear the voice; courageous enough to act on it.

The Fifth Week of Lent
26 March–1 April 2023

Something to think and pray about each day this week:

A friend of mine from the Lutheran tradition has a very interesting question about Catholic Lent. 'Why do you need to do these things once a year – why don't you do all these good things all year?' I must say I had no answer.

When you cut to the quick, there is no doubt that for a Christian the entire year should be Lenten in spirit, but we are frail people and we need a good kick in the backside every so often, and an opportunity to benefit from that self-same kick. In fact, many of the great spiritual writers would hold the view that we should have a Lenten mindset all year round.

Some of these same writers would point out that Lent falls at a time of year when the pantry is running low. When the pantry was all you had, there was a sense of 'making do' until spring produced fresh produce. Lent helped this process. Rather than Lent being an occasion to make a personal decision to give something up it was a chance to live with the reality that the resources of the earth are scarce, and that we live in a fragile world.

Alan Hilliard,
Dipping into Lent

The Presence of God
Dear Jesus, I come to you today longing for your presence. I desire to love you as you love me. May nothing ever separate me from you.

Freedom
Lord, grant me the grace to have freedom of the spirit. Cleanse my heart and soul so that I may live joyously in your love.

Consciousness
Where am I with God? With others?
Do I have something to be grateful for? Then I give thanks.
Is there something I am sorry for? Then I ask forgiveness.

The Word
The word of God comes down to us through the Scriptures. May the Holy Spirit enlighten my mind and my heart to respond to the gospel teachings.
(Please turn to the Scripture on the following pages. Inspiration points are there, should you need them. When you are ready, return here to continue.)

Conversation
How has God's word moved me? Has it left me cold?
Has it consoled me or moved me to act in a new way?
I imagine Jesus standing or sitting beside me;
I turn and share my feelings with him.

Conclusion

I thank God for these moments we have spent together and for any insights I have been given concerning the text.

Sunday 26 March
Fifth Sunday of Lent

John 11:1–45

Now a certain man was ill, Lazarus of Bethany, the village of Mary and her sister Martha. Mary was the one who anointed the Lord with perfume and wiped his feet with her hair; her brother Lazarus was ill. So the sisters sent a message to Jesus, 'Lord, he whom you love is ill.' But when Jesus heard it, he said, 'This illness does not lead to death; rather it is for God's glory, so that the Son of God may be glorified through it.' Accordingly, though Jesus loved Martha and her sister and Lazarus, after having heard that Lazarus was ill, he stayed two days longer in the place where he was.

Then after this he said to the disciples, 'Let us go to Judea again.' The disciples said to him, 'Rabbi, the Jews were just now trying to stone you, and are you going there again?' Jesus answered, 'Are there not twelve hours of daylight? Those who walk during the day do not stumble, because they see the light of this world. But those who walk at night stumble, because the light is not in them.' After saying this, he told them, 'Our friend Lazarus has fallen asleep, but I am going there to awaken him.' The disciples said to him, 'Lord, if he has fallen asleep, he will be all right.' Jesus, however, had been speaking about his death, but they thought that he was referring merely to sleep. Then Jesus told them plainly, 'Lazarus is dead. For your sake I am glad I was not there, so that you may believe. But let us go to him.' Thomas, who was called the Twin, said to his fellow-disciples, 'Let us also go, that we may die with him.'

When Jesus arrived, he found that Lazarus had already been in the tomb for four days. Now Bethany was near Jerusalem, some two miles away, and many of the Jews had come to Martha and Mary to console them about their brother. When Martha heard that Jesus was coming, she went and met him, while Mary stayed at home. Martha said to Jesus, 'Lord, if you had been here, my brother would not have died. But even now I know that God will give you whatever you ask of him.' Jesus said to her, 'Your brother will rise again.' Martha said to him, 'I know that he will rise again in the resurrection on the last day.' Jesus said to her, 'I am the resurrection and the life. Those who believe in me, even though they die, will live, and everyone who lives and believes in me will never die. Do you believe this?' She said to him, 'Yes, Lord, I believe that you are the Messiah, the Son of God, the one coming into the world.'

When she had said this, she went back and called her sister Mary, and told her privately, 'The Teacher is here and is calling for you.' And when she heard it, she got up quickly and went to him. Now Jesus had not yet come to the village, but was still at the place where Martha had met him. The Jews who were with her in the house, consoling her, saw Mary get up quickly and go out. They followed her because they thought that she was going to the tomb to weep there. When Mary came where Jesus was and saw him, she knelt at his feet and said to him, 'Lord, if you had been here, my brother would not have died.' When Jesus saw her weeping, and the Jews who came with her also weeping, he was greatly disturbed in spirit and deeply moved. He said, 'Where have you laid him?' They said to him, 'Lord, come and see.' Jesus began to weep. So the Jews said, 'See how he loved him!' But some of them said, 'Could not he who opened the eyes of the blind man have kept this man from dying?'

Then Jesus, again greatly disturbed, came to the tomb. It was a cave, and a stone was lying against it. Jesus said, 'Take away the stone.' Martha, the sister of the dead man, said to him, 'Lord, already there is a stench because he has been dead for four days.' Jesus said to her, 'Did I not tell you that if you believed, you would see the glory of God?' So they took away the stone. And Jesus looked upwards and said, 'Father, I thank you for having heard me. I knew that you always hear me, but I have said this for the sake of the crowd standing here, so that they may believe that you sent me.' When he had said this, he cried with a loud voice, 'Lazarus, come out!' The dead man came out, his hands and feet bound with strips of cloth, and his face wrapped in a cloth. Jesus said to them, 'Unbind him, and let him go.'

Many of the Jews therefore, who had come with Mary and had seen what Jesus did, believed in him.

- Do I have some sense of being 'dead' in some areas of my life? What is keeping me in the grip of death? Do I have any awareness of what would need to change in my life for me to begin to become more alive again?

Monday 27 March
John 8:2–11

Early in the morning Jesus came again to the temple. All the people came to him and he sat down and began to teach them. The scribes and the Pharisees brought a woman who had been caught in adultery; and making her stand before all of them, they said to him, 'Teacher, this woman was caught in the very act of committing adultery. Now in the law Moses commanded us to stone such women. Now what do you say?' They said this to test him, so that they might have some charge to bring against him. Jesus bent down and wrote with his finger on the ground. When they kept on questioning him, he straightened up and said to them, 'Let anyone among you who is without sin be the first to throw a stone at her.' And once again he bent down and wrote on the ground. When they heard it, they went away, one by one, beginning with the elders; and Jesus was left alone with the woman standing before him. Jesus straightened up and said to her, 'Woman, where are they? Has no one condemned you?' She said, 'No one, sir.' And Jesus said, 'Neither do I condemn you. Go your way, and from now on do not sin again.'

- Have you experienced being challenged for doing something wrong by someone who loves you or by someone who is hostile to you? What has been the difference? To forgive and be forgiven is a wonderful healing.

Tuesday 28 March
John 8:21–30

Again he said to them, 'I am going away, and you will search for me, but you will die in your sin. Where I am going, you cannot come.' Then the Jews said, 'Is he going to kill himself? Is that what he means by saying, "Where I am going, you cannot come"?' He said to them, 'You are from below, I am from above; you are of this world, I am not of this world. I told you that you would die in your sins, for you will die in your sins unless you believe that I am he.' They said to him, 'Who are you?' Jesus said to them, 'Why do I speak to you at all? I have much to say about you and much to condemn; but the one who sent me is true, and I declare to the world what I have heard from him.' They did not understand that he was speaking to them about the Father. So Jesus said, 'When you have lifted up the Son of Man, then you will realise that I am he, and that I do nothing on my own, but I speak these things as the Father instructed me. And the one who sent me is with me; he has not left me alone, for I always do what is pleasing to him.' As he was saying these things, many believed in him.

• Jesus' hearers were either unable or unwilling to understand his teaching up to this point. He is still revealing his identity but he is also explaining the identity of those he is addressing.

Wednesday 29 March
John 8:31–42

Then Jesus said to the Jews who had believed in him, 'If you continue in my word, you are truly my disciples; and you will know the truth, and the truth will make you free.' They answered him, 'We are descendants of Abraham and have never been slaves to anyone. What do you mean by saying, "You will be made free"?'

Jesus answered them, 'Very truly, I tell you, everyone who commits sin is a slave to sin. The slave does not have a permanent place in the household; the son has a place there for ever. So if the Son makes you free, you will be free indeed. I know that you are descendants of Abraham; yet you look for an opportunity to kill me, because there is no place in you for my word. I declare what I have seen in the Father's presence; as for you, you should do what you have heard from the Father.'

They answered him, 'Abraham is our father.' Jesus said to them, 'If you were Abraham's children, you would be doing what Abraham did, but now you are trying to kill me, a man who has told you the truth that I heard from God. This is not what Abraham did. You are indeed doing what your father does.' They said to him, 'We are not illegitimate children; we have one father, God himself.' Jesus said to them, 'If God were your Father, you would love me, for I came from God and now I am here. I did not come on my own, but he sent me.'

- Jesus stresses the importance of keeping his word. Doing this shows that one is a genuine follower of his. It means having the truth – or seeing things like God. This also means being free – from all dark deceptions. There is much to ponder in this.

Thursday 30 March
John 8:51–59

Jesus said to them. 'Very truly, I tell you, whoever keeps my word will never see death.' The Jews said to him, 'Now we know that you have a demon. Abraham died, and so did the prophets; yet you say, "Whoever keeps my word will never taste death." Are you greater than our father Abraham, who died? The prophets also died. Who do you claim to be?' Jesus answered, 'If I glorify myself, my glory is nothing. It is my Father who glorifies me, he of whom you say, "He is our God", though you do not know him. But I know him; if I were to say that I do not know him, I would be a liar like you. But I do know him and I keep his word. Your ancestor Abraham rejoiced that he would see my day; he saw it and was glad.' Then the Jews said to him, 'You are not yet fifty years old, and have you seen Abraham?' Jesus said to them, 'Very truly, I tell you, before Abraham was, I am.' So they picked up stones to throw at him, but Jesus hid himself and went out of the temple.

- The gospel today highlights the difference between the way of Jesus and the way of the authorities. The divine way of looking at things is the deep meaning that Jesus brings to life. His statement 'before Abraham ever was, I Am' pinpoints this difference. Ask Jesus to help you believe in his incarnation as he gives the gift of himself to us.

Friday 31 March

John 10:31–42

The Jews took up stones again to stone him. Jesus replied, 'I have shown you many good works from the Father. For which of these are you going to stone me?'

The Jews answered, 'It is not for a good work that we are going to stone you, but for blasphemy, because you, though only a human being, are making yourself God.' Jesus answered, 'Is it not written in your law, "I said, you are gods"? If those to whom the word of God came were called "gods" – and the scripture cannot be annulled – can you say that the one whom the Father has sanctified and sent into the world is blaspheming because I said, "I am God's Son"? If I am not doing the works of my Father, then do not believe me. But if I do them, even though you do not believe me, believe the works, so that you may know and understand that the Father is in me and I am in the Father.' Then they tried to arrest him again, but he escaped from their hands.

He went away again across the Jordan to the place where John had been baptising earlier, and he remained there. Many came to him, and they were saying, 'John performed no sign, but everything that John said about this man was true.' And many believed in him there.

- The miracles that Jesus was working showed that there was something special about him. They were what the Father had given him to do. They were an indication of a mysterious relationship – that the Father is in him and he is in the Father. This knowledge called for wonder and astonishment. Aren't we all quick to reject and slow to learn?

Saturday 1 April

John 11:45–56

Many of the Jews therefore, who had come with Mary and had seen what Jesus did, believed in him. But some of them went to the Pharisees and told them what he had done. So the chief priests and the Pharisees called a meeting of the council, and said, 'What are we to do? This man is performing many signs. If we let him go on like this, everyone will believe in him, and the Romans will come and destroy both our holy place and our nation.' But one of them, Caiaphas, who was high priest that year, said to them, 'You know nothing at all! You do not understand that it is better for you to have one man die for the people than to have the whole nation destroyed.' He did not say this on his own, but being high priest that year he prophesied that Jesus was about to die for the nation, and not for the nation only, but to gather into one the dispersed children of God. So from that day on they planned to put him to death.

Jesus therefore no longer walked about openly among the Jews, but went from there to a town called Ephraim in the region near the wilderness; and he remained there with the disciples.

Now the Passover of the Jews was near, and many went up from the country to Jerusalem before the Passover to purify themselves. They were looking for

Jesus and were asking one another as they stood in the temple, 'What do you think? Surely he will not come to the festival, will he?'

- I imagine the tension that reigned among Jesus and his group: a few days after their triumphant entry into Jerusalem, they could no longer walk openly in the city without exposing themselves to serious risk. And all this for my sake.

Holy Week
2–8 April 2023

Something to think and pray about each day this week:

Jesus, it seems to me, lived his life in borrowed places.

Born in a borrowed stable, early life lived in a borrowed country, hospitality borrowed from people like Martha, Mary and Lazarus, Passover meal in a borrowed room and death saw him rest in a borrowed tomb. As we reflect on Holy Week, could it be the case he wants to borrow something from you? Something precious and totally your gift to share with him? I think so. He is borrowing not anything you have but all that you are. He is borrowing you! Borrowing you, that like the stable, the foreign country, the friends' home, the Upper Room and the tomb, he may bring something of himself to you in these most sacred days.

Vincent Sherlock,
Celebrating Holy Week

The Presence of God

As I sit here, the beating of my heart,
the ebb and flow of my breathing, the movements of
my mind
are all signs of God's ongoing creation of me.
I pause for a moment and become aware
of this presence of God within me.

Freedom

I will ask God's help
to be free from my own preoccupations,
to be open to God in this time of prayer,
to come to know, love and serve God more.

Consciousness

At this moment, Lord, I turn my thoughts to you.
I will leave aside my chores and preoccupations.
I will take rest and refreshment in your presence.

The Word

Now I turn to the Scripture set out for me this day. I
read slowly over the words and see if any sentence or
sentiment appeals to me.

*(Please turn to the Scripture on the following pages. Inspiration points
are there, should you need them. When you are ready, return here to
continue.)*

Conversation

Begin to talk to Jesus about the Scripture you have just
read. What part of it strikes a chord in you? Perhaps

the words of a friend – or some story you have heard recently – will slowly rise to the surface of your consciousness. If so, does the story throw light on what the Scripture passage may be saying to you?

Conclusion

Glory be to the Father, and to the Son, and to the Holy Spirit,
As it was in the beginning, is now and ever shall be,
World without end. Amen.

Sunday 2 April
Palm Sunday of the Passion of the Lord
Matthew 26:14–27:66

Then one of the twelve, who was called Judas Iscariot, went to the chief priests and said, 'What will you give me if I betray him to you?' They paid him thirty pieces of silver. And from that moment he began to look for an opportunity to betray him.

On the first day of Unleavened Bread the disciples came to Jesus, saying, 'Where do you want us to make the preparations for you to eat the Passover?' He said, 'Go into the city to a certain man, and say to him, "The Teacher says, My time is near; I will keep the Passover at your house with my disciples."' So the disciples did as Jesus had directed them, and they prepared the Passover meal.

When it was evening, he took his place with the twelve; and while they were eating, he said, 'Truly I tell you, one of you will betray me.' And they became greatly distressed and began to say to him one after another, 'Surely not I, Lord?' He answered, 'The one who has dipped his hand into the bowl with me will betray me. The Son of Man goes as it is written of him, but woe to that one by whom the Son of Man is betrayed! It would have been better for that one not to have been born.' Judas, who betrayed him, said, 'Surely not I, Rabbi?' He replied, 'You have said so.'

While they were eating, Jesus took a loaf of bread, and after blessing it he broke it, gave it to the disciples, and said, 'Take, eat; this is my body.' Then he took a cup, and after giving thanks he gave it to them, saying, 'Drink from it, all of you; for this is my blood of the covenant, which is poured out for many for the forgiveness of sins. I tell you, I will never again drink of this fruit of the vine until that day when I drink it new with you in my Father's kingdom.'

When they had sung the hymn, they went out to the Mount of Olives.

Then Jesus said to them, 'You will all become deserters because of me this night; for it is written,

"I will strike the shepherd,
    and the sheep of the flock will be scattered."

But after I am raised up, I will go ahead of you to Galilee.' Peter said to him, 'Though all become deserters because of you, I will never desert you.' Jesus said to him, 'Truly I tell you, this very night, before the cock crows, you will deny me three times.' Peter said to him, 'Even though I must die with you, I will not deny you.' And so said all the disciples.

Then Jesus went with them to a place called Gethsemane; and he said to his disciples, 'Sit here while I go over there and pray.' He took with him Peter and the two sons of Zebedee, and began to be grieved and agitated. Then he said to them, 'I am deeply grieved, even to death; remain here, and stay awake with me.' And going a little farther, he threw himself on the ground and prayed, 'My Father, if it is possible, let this cup pass from me; yet not what I want but what you want.' Then he came to the disciples and found them sleeping; and he said to Peter, 'So, could you not stay awake with me one hour? Stay awake and pray that you may not come into the time of trial; the spirit indeed is willing, but the flesh is weak.' Again he went away for the second time and prayed, 'My Father, if this cannot pass unless I drink it, your will be done.' Again he came and found them sleeping, for their eyes were heavy. So leaving them again, he went away and prayed for the third time, saying the same words. Then he came to the disciples and said to them, 'Are you still sleeping and taking your rest? See, the hour is at hand, and the Son of Man is betrayed into the hands of sinners. Get up, let us be going. See, my betrayer is at hand.'

While he was still speaking, Judas, one of the twelve, arrived; with him was a large crowd with swords and clubs, from the chief priests and the elders of the people. Now the betrayer had given them a sign, saying, 'The one I will kiss is the man; arrest him.' At once he came up to Jesus and said, 'Greetings, Rabbi!' and kissed him. Jesus said to him, 'Friend, do what you are here to do.' Then they came and laid hands on Jesus and arrested him. Suddenly, one of those with

Jesus put his hand on his sword, drew it, and struck the slave of the high priest, cutting off his ear. Then Jesus said to him, 'Put your sword back into its place; for all who take the sword will perish by the sword. Do you think that I cannot appeal to my Father, and he will at once send me more than twelve legions of angels? But how then would the scriptures be fulfilled, which say it must happen in this way?' At that hour Jesus said to the crowds, 'Have you come out with swords and clubs to arrest me as though I were a bandit? Day after day I sat in the temple teaching, and you did not arrest me. But all this has taken place, so that the scriptures of the prophets may be fulfilled.' Then all the disciples deserted him and fled.

Those who had arrested Jesus took him to Caiaphas the high priest, in whose house the scribes and the elders had gathered. But Peter was following him at a distance, as far as the courtyard of the high priest; and going inside, he sat with the guards in order to see how this would end. Now the chief priests and the whole council were looking for false testimony against Jesus so that they might put him to death, but they found none, though many false witnesses came forward. At last two came forward and said, 'This fellow said, "I am able to destroy the temple of God and to build it in three days."' The high priest stood up and said, 'Have you no answer? What is it that they testify against you?' But Jesus was silent. Then the high priest said to him, 'I put you under oath before the living God, tell us if you are the Messiah, the Son of God.' Jesus said to him, 'You have said so. But I tell you,

> From now on you will see the Son of Man
>> seated at the right hand of Power
>> and coming on the clouds of heaven.'

Then the high priest tore his clothes and said, 'He has blasphemed! Why do we still need witnesses? You have now heard his blasphemy. What is your verdict?' They answered, 'He deserves death.' Then they spat in his face and struck him; and some slapped him, saying, 'Prophesy to us, you Messiah! Who is it that struck you?'

Now Peter was sitting outside in the courtyard. A servant-girl came to him and said, 'You also were with Jesus the Galilean.' But he denied it before all of them, saying, 'I do not know what you are talking about.' When he went out to the porch, another servant-girl saw him, and she said to the bystanders, 'This man was with Jesus of Nazareth.' Again he denied it with an oath, 'I do not know the man.' After a little while the bystanders came up and said to Peter, 'Certainly you are also one of them, for your accent betrays you.' Then he began to curse, and he swore an oath, 'I do not know the man!' At that moment the cock crowed. Then Peter remembered what Jesus had said: 'Before the cock crows, you will deny me three times.' And he went out and wept bitterly.

When morning came, all the chief priests and the elders of the people conferred together against Jesus in order to bring about his death. They bound him, led him away, and handed him over to Pilate the governor.

When Judas, his betrayer, saw that Jesus was condemned, he repented and brought back the thirty pieces of silver to the chief priests and the elders. He said, 'I have sinned by betraying innocent blood.' But they said, 'What is that to us? See to it yourself.' Throwing down the pieces of silver in the temple, he departed; and he went and hanged himself. But the chief priests, taking the pieces of silver, said, 'It is not lawful to put them into the treasury, since they are blood money.' After conferring together, they used them to buy the potter's field as a place to bury foreigners. For this reason that field has been called the Field of Blood to this day. Then was fulfilled what had been spoken through the prophet Jeremiah, 'And they took the thirty pieces of silver, the price of the one on whom a price had been set, on whom some of the people of Israel had set a price, and they gave them for the potter's field, as the Lord commanded me.'

Now Jesus stood before the governor; and the governor asked him, 'Are you the King of the Jews?' Jesus said, 'You say so.' But when he was accused by the chief priests and elders, he did not answer. Then

Pilate said to him, 'Do you not hear how many accusations they make against you?' But he gave him no answer, not even to a single charge, so that the governor was greatly amazed.

Now at the festival the governor was accustomed to release a prisoner for the crowd, anyone whom they wanted. At that time they had a notorious prisoner, called Jesus Barabbas. So after they had gathered, Pilate said to them, 'Whom do you want me to release for you, Jesus Barabbas or Jesus who is called the Messiah?' For he realised that it was out of jealousy that they had handed him over. While he was sitting on the judgement seat, his wife sent word to him, 'Have nothing to do with that innocent man, for today I have suffered a great deal because of a dream about him.' Now the chief priests and the elders persuaded the crowds to ask for Barabbas and to have Jesus killed. The governor again said to them, 'Which of the two do you want me to release for you?' And they said, 'Barabbas.' Pilate said to them, 'Then what should I do with Jesus who is called the Messiah?' All of them said, 'Let him be crucified!' Then he asked, 'Why, what evil has he done?' But they shouted all the more, 'Let him be crucified!'

So when Pilate saw that he could do nothing, but rather that a riot was beginning, he took some water and washed his hands before the crowd, saying, 'I am innocent of this man's blood; see to it yourselves.'

Then the people as a whole answered, 'His blood be on us and on our children!' So he released Barabbas for them; and after flogging Jesus, he handed him over to be crucified.

Then the soldiers of the governor took Jesus into the governor's headquarters, and they gathered the whole cohort around him. They stripped him and put a scarlet robe on him, and after twisting some thorns into a crown, they put it on his head. They put a reed in his right hand and knelt before him and mocked him, saying, 'Hail, King of the Jews!' They spat on him, and took the reed and struck him on the head. After mocking him, they stripped him of the robe and put his own clothes on him. Then they led him away to crucify him.

As they went out, they came upon a man from Cyrene named Simon; they compelled this man to carry his cross. And when they came to a place called Golgotha (which means Place of a Skull), they offered him wine to drink, mixed with gall; but when he tasted it, he would not drink it. And when they had crucified him, they divided his clothes among themselves by casting lots; then they sat down there and kept watch over him. Over his head they put the charge against him, which read, 'This is Jesus, the King of the Jews.'

Then two bandits were crucified with him, one on his right and one on his left. Those who passed by derided him, shaking their heads and saying, 'You who would destroy the temple and build it in three days, save yourself! If you are the Son of God, come down from the cross.' In the same way the chief priests also, along with the scribes and elders, were mocking him, saying, 'He saved others; he cannot save himself. He is the King of Israel; let him come down from the cross now, and we will believe in him. He trusts in God; let God deliver him now, if he wants to; for he said, "I am God's Son."' The bandits who were crucified with him also taunted him in the same way.

From noon on, darkness came over the whole land until three in the afternoon. And about three o'clock Jesus cried with a loud voice, 'Eli, Eli, lama sabachthani?' that is, 'My God, my God, why have you forsaken me?' When some of the bystanders heard it, they said, 'This man is calling for Elijah.' At once one of them ran and got a sponge, filled it with sour wine, put it on a stick, and gave it to him to drink. But the others said, 'Wait, let us see whether Elijah will come to save him.' Then Jesus cried again with a loud voice and breathed his last. At that moment the curtain of the temple was torn in two, from top to bottom. The earth shook, and the rocks were split. The tombs also were opened, and many bodies of the saints who had fallen asleep were raised. After his resurrection they came out of the tombs and entered the holy city and appeared to many. Now when the centurion and those with him, who were keeping watch over Jesus, saw the earthquake and what took place, they were terrified and said, 'Truly this man was God's Son!'

Many women were also there, looking on from a distance; they had followed Jesus from Galilee and had provided for him. Among them were Mary Magdalene, and Mary the mother of James and Joseph, and the mother of the sons of Zebedee.

When it was evening, there came a rich man from Arimathea, named Joseph, who was also a disciple of Jesus. He went to Pilate and asked for the body of Jesus; then Pilate ordered it to be given to him. So Joseph took the body and wrapped it in a clean linen cloth and laid it in his own new tomb, which he had hewn in the rock. He then rolled a great stone to the door of the tomb and went away. Mary Magdalene and the other Mary were there, sitting opposite the tomb.

The next day, that is, after the day of Preparation, the chief priests and the Pharisees gathered before Pilate and said, 'Sir, we remember what that impostor said while he was still alive, "After three days I will rise again." Therefore command that the tomb be made secure until the third day; otherwise his disciples may go and steal him away, and tell the people, "He has been raised from the dead", and the last deception would be worse than the first.' Pilate said to them, 'You have a guard of soldiers; go, make it as secure as you can.' So they went with the guard and made the tomb secure by sealing the stone.

- The concept of betrayal, referenced here five times, is central in the Passion. Recall an experience you have had of being betrayed – perhaps you were let down by a friend, or a partner, or perhaps like many Catholics today you feel let down by the Church. How did you react? Did you retaliate, walk away or do your best to forgive?

Monday 3 April

John 12:1–11

Six days before the Passover Jesus came to Bethany, the home of Lazarus, whom he had raised from the dead. There they gave a dinner for him. Martha served, and Lazarus was one of those at the table with him. Mary took a pound of costly perfume made of pure nard, anointed Jesus' feet, and wiped them with her hair. The house was filled with the fragrance of the perfume. But Judas Iscariot, one of his disciples (the one who was about to betray him), said, 'Why was this perfume not sold for three hundred denarii and the money given to the poor?' (He said this not because he cared about the poor, but because he was a thief; he kept the common purse and used to steal what was put into it.) Jesus said, 'Leave her alone. She bought it so that she might keep it for the day of my burial. You always have the poor with you, but you do not always have me.'

When the great crowd of the Jews learned that he was there, they came not only because of Jesus but also to see Lazarus, whom he had raised from the dead. So the chief priests planned to put Lazarus to death as well, since it was on account of him that many of the Jews were deserting and were believing in Jesus.

- Mary is praying with her body and with her heart. It is a way we seldom pray. Her prayer is part of a tradition as old as the passionate, lyrical and sensuous Song of Solomon. Yet there is nothing to stop us praying this way – a gentle touch of understanding, a hug of reassurance, a smile of love – these, too, are prayers.

Tuesday 4 April
John 13:21–33, 36–38

After saying this Jesus was troubled in spirit, and declared, 'Very truly, I tell you, one of you will betray me.' The disciples looked at one another, uncertain of whom he was speaking. One of his disciples – the one whom Jesus loved – was reclining next to him; Simon Peter therefore motioned to him to ask Jesus of whom he was speaking. So while reclining next to Jesus, he asked him, 'Lord, who is it?' Jesus answered, 'It is the one to whom I give this piece of bread when I have dipped it in the dish.' So when he had dipped the piece of bread, he gave it to Judas son of Simon

Iscariot. After he received the piece of bread, Satan entered into him. Jesus said to him, 'Do quickly what you are going to do.' Now no one at the table knew why he said this to him. Some thought that, because Judas had the common purse, Jesus was telling him, 'Buy what we need for the festival'; or, that he should give something to the poor. So, after receiving the piece of bread, he immediately went out. And it was night.

When he had gone out, Jesus said, 'Now the Son of Man has been glorified, and God has been glorified in him. If God has been glorified in him, God will also glorify him in himself and will glorify him at once. Little children, I am with you only a little longer. You will look for me; and as I said to the Jews so now I say to you, "Where I am going, you cannot come."'

Simon Peter said to him, 'Lord, where are you going?' Jesus answered, 'Where I am going, you cannot follow me now; but you will follow afterwards.' Peter said to him, 'Lord, why can I not follow you now? I will lay down my life for you.' Jesus answered, 'Will you lay down your life for me? Very truly, I tell you, before the cock crows, you will have denied me three times.'

- Christ tells his disciples that he is going away, and that for the moment they cannot come with him. Peter asserts that he will be with Jesus come what may, but he is unaware of his own frailty. Our good intentions are often not carried out.

Wednesday 5 April
Matthew 26:14–25

Then one of the twelve, who was called Judas Iscariot, went to the chief priests and said, 'What will you give me if I betray him to you?' They paid him thirty pieces of silver. And from that moment he began to look for an opportunity to betray him.

On the first day of Unleavened Bread the disciples came to Jesus, saying, 'Where do you want us to make the preparations for you to eat the Passover?' He said, 'Go into the city to a certain man, and say to him, "The Teacher says, My time is near; I will keep the Passover at your house with my disciples."' So the disciples did as Jesus had directed them, and they prepared the Passover meal.

When it was evening, he took his place with the twelve; and while they were eating, he said, 'Truly I tell you, one of you will betray me.' And they became greatly distressed and began to say to him one after another, 'Surely not I, Lord?' He answered, 'The one who has dipped his hand into the bowl with me will betray me. The Son of Man goes as it is written of him, but woe to that one by whom the Son of Man is betrayed! It would have been better for that one not to have been born.' Judas, who betrayed him, said, 'Surely not I, Rabbi?' He replied, 'You have said so.'

- Holy Week is an invitation to walk closely with Jesus: we fix our gaze on him and accompany him in his suffering; we let him look closely at us and see us as we really are. We do not have to present a brave face to him, but can tell him about where we have been disappointed, let down – perhaps even betrayed. We avoid getting stuck in our own misfortune by seeing as he sees, by learning from his heart.

Thursday 6 April
Holy Thursday

John 13:1–15

Now before the festival of the Passover, Jesus knew that his hour had come to depart from this world and go to the Father. Having loved his own who were in the world, he loved them to the end. The devil had already put it into the heart of Judas son of Simon Iscariot to betray him. And during supper Jesus, knowing that the Father had given all things into his hands, and that he had come from God and was going to God, got up from the table, took off his outer robe, and tied a towel around himself. Then he poured water into a basin and began to wash the disciples' feet and to wipe them with the towel that was tied around him. He came to Simon Peter, who said to him, 'Lord, are you going to wash my feet?' Jesus answered, 'You do not know now what I am doing, but later you will understand.'

Peter said to him, 'You will never wash my feet.' Jesus answered, 'Unless I wash you, you have no share with me.' Simon Peter said to him, 'Lord, not my feet only but also my hands and my head!' Jesus said to him, 'One who has bathed does not need to wash, except for the feet, but is entirely clean. And you are clean, though not all of you.' For he knew who was to betray him; for this reason he said, 'Not all of you are clean.'

After he had washed their feet, had put on his robe, and had returned to the table, he said to them, 'Do you know what I have done to you? You call me Teacher and Lord – and you are right, for that is what I am. So if I, your Lord and Teacher, have washed your feet, you also ought to wash one another's feet. For I have set you an example, that you also should do as I have done to you.'

• Do I feel like Peter, when Jesus kneels at my feet? Let me hear him whisper to me: 'Unless I wash you, you have no share with me.' Have I the courage and the generosity to accept his humble service and unconditional love?

Friday 7 April
Good Friday
John 18:1–19:42

After Jesus had spoken these words, he went out with his disciples across the Kidron valley to a place where there was a garden, which he and his disciples entered. Now Judas, who betrayed him, also knew the place, because Jesus often met there with his disciples. So Judas brought a detachment of soldiers together with police from the chief priests and the Pharisees, and they came there with lanterns and torches and weapons. Then Jesus, knowing all that was to happen to him, came forward and asked them, 'For whom are you looking?' They answered, 'Jesus of Nazareth.' Jesus replied, 'I am he.' Judas, who betrayed him, was standing with them. When Jesus said to them, 'I am he', they stepped back and fell to the ground. Again he asked them, 'For whom are you looking?' And they said, 'Jesus of Nazareth.' Jesus answered, 'I told you that I am he. So if you are looking for me, let these men go.' This was to fulfil the word that he had spoken, 'I did not lose a single one of those whom you gave me.' Then Simon Peter, who had a sword, drew it, struck the high priest's slave, and cut off his right ear. The slave's name was Malchus. Jesus said to Peter, 'Put your sword back into its sheath. Am I not to drink the cup that the Father has given me?'

So the soldiers, their officer, and the Jewish police arrested Jesus and bound him. First they took him to Annas, who was the father-in-law of Caiaphas, the high priest that year. Caiaphas was the one who had advised the Jews that it was better to have one person die for the people.

Simon Peter and another disciple followed Jesus. Since that disciple was known to the high priest, he went with Jesus into the courtyard of the high priest, but Peter was standing outside at the gate. So the other disciple, who was known to the high priest, went out, spoke to the woman who guarded the gate, and brought Peter in. The woman said to Peter, 'You are not also one of this man's disciples, are you?' He said, 'I am not.' Now the slaves and the police had made a charcoal fire because it was cold, and they were standing round it and warming themselves. Peter also was standing with them and warming himself.

Then the high priest questioned Jesus about his disciples and about his teaching. Jesus answered, 'I have spoken openly to the world; I have always taught in synagogues and in the temple, where all the Jews come together. I have said nothing in secret. Why do you ask me? Ask those who heard what I said to them; they know what I said.' When he had said this, one of the police standing nearby struck Jesus on the face, saying, 'Is that how you answer the high priest?' Jesus answered, 'If I have spoken wrongly, testify to the wrong. But if I have spoken rightly, why do you strike me?' Then Annas sent him bound to Caiaphas the high priest.

Now Simon Peter was standing and warming himself. They asked him, 'You are not also one of his disciples, are you?' He denied it and said, 'I am not.'

One of the slaves of the high priest, a relative of the man whose ear Peter had cut off, asked, 'Did I not see you in the garden with him?' Again Peter denied it, and at that moment the cock crowed.

Then they took Jesus from Caiaphas to Pilate's headquarters. It was early in the morning. They themselves did not enter the headquarters, so as to avoid ritual defilement and to be able to eat the Passover. So Pilate went out to them and said, 'What accusation do you bring against this man?' They answered, 'If this man were not a criminal, we would not have handed him over to you.' Pilate said to them, 'Take him yourselves and judge him according to your law.' The Jews replied, 'We are not permitted to put anyone to death.' (This was to fulfil what Jesus had said when he indicated the kind of death he was to die.)

Then Pilate entered the headquarters again, summoned Jesus, and asked him, 'Are you the King of the Jews?' Jesus answered, 'Do you ask this on your own, or did others tell you about me?' Pilate replied, 'I am not a Jew, am I? Your own nation and the chief priests have handed you over to me. What have you done?' Jesus answered, 'My kingdom is not from this world. If my kingdom were from this world, my followers would be fighting to keep me from being handed over to the Jews. But as it is, my kingdom is not from here.' Pilate asked him, 'So you are a king?' Jesus answered, 'You say that I am a king. For this I was born, and for this I came into the world, to testify to the truth. Everyone who belongs to the truth listens to my voice.' Pilate asked him, 'What is truth?'

After he had said this, he went out to the Jews again and told them, 'I find no case against him. But you have a custom that I release someone for you at the Passover. Do you want me to release for you the King of the Jews?' They shouted in reply, 'Not this man, but Barabbas!' Now Barabbas was a bandit.

Then Pilate took Jesus and had him flogged. And the soldiers wove a crown of thorns and put it on his head, and they dressed him in a purple robe. They kept coming up to him, saying, 'Hail, King of the Jews!' and striking him on the face. Pilate went out again and said to them, 'Look, I am bringing him out to you to let you know that I find no case against him.' So Jesus came out, wearing the crown of thorns and the purple robe. Pilate said to them, 'Here is the man!' When the chief priests and the police saw him, they shouted, 'Crucify him! Crucify him!' Pilate said to them, 'Take him yourselves and crucify him; I find no case against him.' The Jews answered him, 'We have a law, and according to that law he ought to die because he has claimed to be the Son of God.'

Now when Pilate heard this, he was more afraid than ever. He entered his headquarters again and asked Jesus, 'Where are you from?' But Jesus gave him no answer. Pilate therefore said to him, 'Do you refuse to speak to me? Do you not know that I have power to release you, and power to crucify you?' Jesus answered him, 'You would have no power over me unless it had been given you from above; therefore the one who handed me over to you is guilty of a greater sin.' From then on Pilate tried to release him, but the Jews cried out, 'If you release this man, you are no friend of the emperor. Everyone who claims to be a king sets himself against the emperor.'

When Pilate heard these words, he brought Jesus outside and sat on the judge's bench at a place called The Stone Pavement, or in Hebrew Gabbatha. Now it was the day of Preparation for the Passover; and it was about noon. He said to the Jews, 'Here is your King!' They cried out, 'Away with him! Away with him! Crucify him!' Pilate asked them, 'Shall I crucify your King?' The chief priests answered, 'We have no king but the emperor.' Then he handed him over to them to be crucified.

So they took Jesus; and carrying the cross by himself, he went out to what is called The Place of the Skull, which in Hebrew is called Golgotha. There they crucified him, and with him two others, one on either side, with Jesus between them. Pilate also had an inscription written and put on the cross. It read, 'Jesus of Nazareth, the King of the Jews.' Many of the Jews read this inscription, because the place where Jesus was crucified was near the city; and it was written in Hebrew, in Latin and in Greek. Then the chief priests of the Jews said to Pilate, 'Do not write, "The King of the Jews", but, "This man said, I am King of the Jews."' Pilate answered, 'What I have written I have written.' When the soldiers had crucified Jesus, they took his clothes and divided them into four parts, one for each soldier. They also took his tunic; now the tunic was seamless, woven in one piece from the top. So they said to one another, 'Let us not tear it, but cast lots for it to see who will get it.' This was to fulfil what the scripture says,

> 'They divided my clothes among themselves,
>   and for my clothing they cast lots.'

And that is what the soldiers did.

Meanwhile, standing near the cross of Jesus were his mother, and his mother's sister, Mary the wife of Clopas, and Mary Magdalene. When Jesus saw his mother and the disciple whom he loved standing beside her, he said to his mother, 'Woman, here is your son.' Then he said to the disciple, 'Here is your mother.' And from that hour the disciple took her into his own home.

After this, when Jesus knew that all was now finished, he said (in order to fulfil the scripture), 'I am thirsty.' A jar full of sour wine was standing there. So they put a sponge full of the wine on a branch of hyssop and held it to his mouth. When Jesus had received the wine, he said, 'It is finished.' Then he bowed his head and gave up his spirit.

Since it was the day of Preparation, the Jews did not want the bodies left on the cross during the sabbath, especially because that sabbath was a day of great solemnity. So they asked Pilate to have the legs of the crucified men broken and the bodies removed. Then the soldiers came and broke the legs of the first and of the other who had been crucified with him. But when they came to Jesus and saw that he was already dead, they did not break his legs. Instead, one of the soldiers pierced his side with a spear, and at once blood and water came out. (He who saw this has testified so that you also may believe. His testimony is true, and he knows that he tells the truth.) These things occurred so that the scripture might be fulfilled, 'None of his bones shall be broken.' And again another passage of scripture says, 'They will look on the one whom they have pierced.'

After these things, Joseph of Arimathea, who was a disciple of Jesus, though a secret one because of his fear of the Jews, asked Pilate to let him take away the body of Jesus. Pilate gave him permission; so he came and removed his body. Nicodemus, who had at first come to Jesus by night, also came, bringing a mixture of myrrh and aloes, weighing about a hundred pounds. They took the body of Jesus and wrapped it with the spices in linen cloths, according to the burial custom of the Jews. Now there was a garden in the place where he was crucified, and in the garden there was a new tomb in which no one had ever been laid. And so, because it was the Jewish day of Preparation, and the tomb was nearby, they laid Jesus there.

• They took Jesus to Calvary and crucified him there. It looked a brutal act, but what splendour was shining through it! The cross ever stands as a symbol of power in weakness. The thirst of Christ on the cross is only a mirror of the depths of his prayer and longing.

Saturday 8 April
Holy Saturday
Matthew 28:1–10

After the sabbath, as the first day of the week was dawning, Mary Magdalene and the other Mary went to see the tomb. And suddenly there was a great earthquake; for an angel of the Lord, descending from heaven, came and rolled back the stone and sat on it. His appearance was like lightning, and his clothing white as snow. For fear of him the guards shook and became like dead men. But the angel said to the women, 'Do not be afraid; I know that you are looking for Jesus who was crucified. He is not here; for he has been raised, as he said. Come, see the place where he lay. Then go quickly and tell his disciples,

"He has been raised from the dead, and indeed he is going ahead of you to Galilee; there you will see him." This is my message for you.' So they left the tomb quickly with fear and great joy, and ran to tell his disciples. Suddenly Jesus met them and said, 'Greetings!' And they came to him, took hold of his feet, and worshipped him. Then Jesus said to them, 'Do not be afraid; go and tell my brothers to go to Galilee; there they will see me.'

- It cannot but impress us that the Gospels, which provide such a detailed account of the Passion, do not contain one single word describing the Resurrection. We only read of the women going to the tomb and finding it empty. They are told that Jesus is not there, for he is risen. You will meet him in Galilee, in the land of your ordinary life. I pray to be able to find him in my life, for he is already there.

Sunday 9 April
Easter Sunday of the Resurrection of the Lord

John 20:1–9

Early on the first day of the week, while it was still dark, Mary Magdalene came to the tomb and saw that the stone had been removed from the tomb. So she ran and went to Simon Peter and the other disciple, the one whom Jesus loved, and said to them, 'They have taken the Lord out of the tomb, and we do not know where they have laid him.' Then Peter and the other disciple set out and went towards the tomb. The two were running together, but the other disciple out-ran Peter and reached the tomb first. He bent down to look in and saw the linen wrappings lying there, but he did not go in. Then Simon Peter came, follow-ing him, and went into the tomb. He saw the linen wrappings lying there, and the cloth that had been on Jesus' head, not lying with the linen wrappings but rolled up in a place by itself. Then the other disciple, who reached the tomb first, also went in, and he saw and believed; for as yet they did not understand the scripture, that he must rise from the dead.

- This is the day that the Lord has made, let us re-joice and be glad. Jesus is risen, never to die again. After the anguish of the last few days, it is the time of unbounded joy. I ask for the grace to enter into the joy of Jesus himself, the seed that fell to the ground and died, and is now bearing abundant fruit, full of new life.

Suscipe

Take, Lord, and receive all my liberty,
my memory, my understanding,
and my entire will,

all I have and call my own.
You have given all to me.

To you, Lord, I return it.
Everything is yours; do with it what you will.
Give me only your love and your grace;
that is enough for me.

—St. Ignatius of Loyola

Prayer to Know God's Will

May it please the supreme and divine Goodness
To give us all abundant grace
Ever to know his most holy will
And perfectly to fulfill it.

—St. Ignatius of Loyola